LABORUM DULCE LENIMEN

G. SCHIRMER

KABALEVSKY
SELECTED PIANO PIECES
Elementary to Upper Elementary Level

29 Pieces from Op. 27, Op. 39 and Op. 89
in Progressive Order

Compiled and Edited by Richard Walters

The pieces were previously published in the following
Schirmer Performance Editions volumes:

Kabalevsky: 30 Pieces for Children, Op. 27
edited by Richard Walters

Kabalevsky: 24 Pieces for Children, Op. 39
edited by Margaret Otwell

Kabalevsky: 35 Easy Pieces, Op. 89
edited by Richard Walters

The fingerings for selections from opus 27
and opus 39 are editorial suggestions;
the fingerings for selections from opus 89
are by the composer.

On the cover:
Murnau (1908)
by Wassily Kandinsky (1866–1944)

ISBN 978-1-4950-8881-0

G. SCHIRMER, *Inc.*

DISTRIBUTED BY
HAL•LEONARD®
7777 W. BLUEMOUND RD. P.O. BOX 13819 MILWAUKEE, WI 53213

www.musicsalesclassical.com
www.halleonard.com

CONTENTS

*Though presented by opus number on the table contents,
the music is presented in progressive order of difficulty*

HISTORICAL NOTES

Dmitri Kabalevsky (1904–1987)

"Art shapes the man, his heart and mind, his feelings and convictions—the whole of his spiritual world. More than that art influences the development of society." —Dmitri Kabalevsky

Kabalevsky was born in St. Petersburg the son of a mathematician. Dmitri not only learned to play the piano, but also was a competent poet and painter as well. Facing financial difficulties, the family moved to Moscow following the October Revolution of 1917. Economic conditions in Russia were dire following World War I. In the ensuing political upheaval, work was hard to find. The Kabalevskys struggled as part of the working poor. Dmitri assisted in bringing in income, beginning to give piano lessons at 15 and playing for silent films at the theatre. He also held odd jobs, including delivering mail and drawing placards for shop windows.

In 1918, Kabalevsky began studying piano and art at the Scriabin Institute. His father wanted him to focus on economics and become a mathematician, but music quickly won the young boy's passions. He soon began teaching at the institute. Kabalevsky enrolled at the Moscow Conservatory in 1925, studying composition and piano.

At the conservatory Kabalevsky joined two musical groups. The Proizvodstvennyi Kollektiv was a conservative, pro-Lenin organization. The Association of Contemporary Musicians was a progressive, avant-garde group. Hardly ten years after the Revolution and the uncertainty of political stability, Kabalevsky deliberately formed relationships with both political camps. This diplomacy would make him one of the most powerful musical voices in the USSR.

Kabalevsky graduated from the conservatory in 1930 and began lecturing there soon after. In 1932, when the Communist Party dissolved all music organizations and created the Union of Soviet Composers, Kabalevsky stepped up as a founding member, using his ties with the more conservative

Proizvodstvennyi Kollektiv to demonstrate his commitment to traditional Russian values and the Russian people. He became a writer for the magazine *Muzgiz* and for *Moscow Radio*. These platforms allowed him to endorse Russian music that was "for the people" and condemn the music that was overly "formalist," a catch-all phrase used by Communist leaders to identify art intended for the "intellectual connoisseurs or sophisticated esoterics," ideas the Communists lifted almost directly from Tolstoy's *What is Art?*

Kabalevsky married in 1931, divorced in 1935, and remarried in 1937. During this time, in addition to his continued teaching appointment at the Moscow Conservatory, he became the senior editor of *Muzgiz*. In 1939, he gained full professorship at the conservatory. Throughout the 1930s, Kabalevsky began to take a more prominent role in the Union of Soviet Composers and in the 1940s, became editor of the *Sovetskaya Muzika*, as well as the Chief of the Board of Feature Broadcasting on *Moscow Radio* after joining the Communist Party. The Soviet government considered him important enough to be evacuated during World War II to Sverdlovsk (now Yekaterinburg) as Hitler's army drew closer to Moscow.

Following World War II, the Conference of Musicians at the Central Committee of the All-Union Communist Party was held in 1948 to outline a policy known as Socialist Realism, the official name of Marxist art and aesthetic theory. The policy asked artists to create art that is "comprehensible to the masses, and inspires the people with admiration for the dignity of the working man and his task of building Communism."[1] The conference and ensuing policy spawned widespread questioning of anyone whose music was not politically correct. There were interrogations and threats to those who would not change their style to serve the party. Somehow Kabalevsky managed to get his name removed from the list of potentially "harmful" composers. He is the only prominent Russian composer of the time to avoid interrogation.

Kabalevsky published just over 100 pieces and wrote far more during his life. Most famous today are his suite *The Comedians*, his violin concerto, and several piano collections. The style is always conservative, approachable, and clear, yet quirky, inventive, and light-hearted. Kabalevsky's music demonstrates a master composer capable of disciplined and limited use of material based on a few fundamentals, like a painter that deliberately uses a limited palate of colors.

Beginning in the 1950s until his death, Kabalevsky wrote little music. Instead, he became heavily involved in national and international pedagogical organizations. From 1952 until his death he served on the board of the Union of Soviet Composers of the USSR; in 1953 he became a member of the Soviet Committee for the Defense of Peace; in 1954, USSR Ministry of Culture; in 1955, World Peace Council; in 1961, United Nations Educational, Scientific and Cultural Organization International Music Council, Council of Directors of the International Society for Music Education. Later, he became a member of the Committee for Lenin Prizes for Literature and Art, the Head of the Council on Aesthetic Education, a deputy to the USSR Supreme Council, Honorary President of the Academy of Pedagogical Sciences in the USSR, and Honorary President of the International Society of Music Education.

During much of this time, Kabalevsky also gave lectures on radio, television, and at various functions in many different countries on music appreciation, pedagogy, and aesthetics.

Perhaps Kabalevsky's most enduring contribution to Soviet music education was his work with the Laboratory of Musical Education in the 1970s. He succeeded in compiling specific lesson plans to be implemented in all Soviet classrooms. It became a complete syllabus (texts, recordings, and detailed outlines of each lesson) for all music education in the country. He then went into the primary schools of Moscow to implement this system. The program focused on political indoctrination, moral education, and character training at its base. Eventually Kabalevsky retired from the conservatory and dedicated his full attention to the education of children in primary schools. He stated in 1974, "when I decided it was time to sum up my work in this [music education] field, I discovered that it was not the summing up, but the beginning of a new stage. I realized that all I had done was merely preparation for going into general schools not merely as a composer or lecturer, but as an ordinary teacher of music."[2]

Up to the last moments of his life Kabalevsky was furthering music education and peaceful relations between all people of all cultures. He died of a heart attack at a conference at which he was to deliver a lecture on the disarmament of world powers of their nuclear weapons.

In Frank Callaway's eulogy given a few days later, he summed up the great influence of the composer: "Kabalevsky believed and demonstrated that music cultivates the artistic tastes and the creative imagination of children, as well as their love of life, of people, of nature, of motherland, and fosters their interest in, and friendships toward, peoples of all nations."[3]

---

[1] David Lawrence Forrest, *The Educational Theory of Dmitri Kabalevsky in Relation to His Piano Music for Children* (Ph.D. diss., University of Melbourne. 1996), 87.

[2] ibid., 36.

[3] ibid., 40.

INTRODUCTION TO KABALEVSKY'S MUSIC

"We live in a difficult—interesting but difficult—epoch, but still life is wonderful. Great art can only come from love for life, love for man. Art must serve society, the people must understand it. The love of man must be there." —Dmitri Kabalevsky.[1]

In his book *Music and Education: A Composer Writes About Musical Education*, Kabalevsky several times cites the quotation by Maxim Gorki that books for children should be "the same as for adults, only better."[2] This quotation is the guiding principle behind all of Kabalevsky's music for children. He did not want to compose simplified or dumbed-down adult art, but good art for children. This flowed very naturally out of his educational theories, that of teaching musical literacy rather than musical grammar, instructing how to listen to music, define shapes and structures, not just how to read or how to identify elements of music.

Building an educational framework, Kabalevsky's book *A Story of Three Whales and Many Other Things* identifies three archetypes as basic musical forms from which all other larger forms are generated and most accessible to children: song, dance, and march. The archetypes (or whales) become the bridges upon which children may enter the world of music. Nearly all of Kabalevsky's music for children can be understood as fitting into one of these categories.

Kabalevsky believed that "no piece of music, however short and modest, should pass by a child without touching his mind and heart."[3] And it is easy to hear in his pedagogical works that he was focusing on developing a real musical understanding in children rather than just getting them to practice or learn scales.

Kabalevsky composed 253 pieces during his lifetime. There are 26 sonatas, sets or suites of piano music, from concert level works for advanced players to 153 pieces specifically written for progressing piano students. It is no wonder he has remained such a popular choice among piano teachers.

It is worth saying that Kabalevsky considered music to be for people of all ages. His specific emphasis was on creating good music first, then helping students understand the music. Even though some of the titles of his works refer to children, they continue in the tradition established by composers like Schumann and Tchaikovsky in creating well-crafted, approachable pieces that focus on specific pedagogical techniques that piano students of any age will find valuable.

[1] in an interview with *The New York Times*, October 27, 1957 "Optimistic Russian: Kabalevsky, in Speaking of His Fourth Symphony, Reveals Attitude to Life" (quoted in Forrest, 103).

[2] Dmitri Kabalevsky, *Music and Education: A Composer Writes About Musical Education* (London: Jessica Kingsley Publishers, 1988), 120.

[3] David Lawrence Forrest, *The Educational Theory of Dmitri Kabalevsky in Relation to His Piano Music for Children* (Ph.D. diss., University of Melbourne. 1996), 143.

References

Daragan, Dina Grigor'yevna. "Kabalevsky, Dmitry Borisovich," *The New Grove Dictionary of Music and Musicians*. ed. S. Sadie and J. Tyrrell. London: Macmillan. 2001.

Forrest, David Lawrence. *The Educational Theory of Dmitri Kabalevsky in Relation to His Piano Music for Children*. (Ph.D. diss., University of Melbourne. 1996).

Kabalevsky, Dimitri. *Music and Education: A Composer Writes About Musical Education*. London: Jessica Kingsley Publishers, 1988.

Krebs, Stanley Dale. *Soviet Composers and the Development of Soviet Music*. New York: W. W. Norton & Company, 1970.

Maes Francis. trans. Arnold J. and Erica Pomerans. *A History of Russian Music: From Kamarinskaya to Babi Yar*. Berkley: University of California Press, 2002.

—Richard Walters, editor
and Joshua Parman, assistant editor

ABOUT THE INDIVIDUAL PIECES
in order by opus number

24 Pieces for Children, Op. 39 is similar to *35 Easy Pieces,* Op. 89, composed almost 30 years later. Both sets start with beginner level pieces and move progressively up to what could be called an early intermediate level. *30 Pieces for Children,* Op. 27, begins at a bit higher level, probably what could generally be called early intermediate, and progresses up to upper intermediate or slightly beyond.

Selections from *30 Pieces for Children,* Op. 27
composed 1937–38 (slightly revised 1985)

Waltz (No. 1)

Practice and Performance Tips
- The quiet, treble range of the piece reminds one of a music box.
- Feel the tempo in whole measures with the lilt of a waltz, rather than individual beats.
- Practice hands together slowly.
- The entire piece is built on two-note slurs. These should be played cleanly and gracefully.
- In the right hand the two-note slur ends in a sustained quarter note. Do not clip this quarter note too short, which would destroy the *cantabile* of the right-hand melody.
- In the left hand the two-note slur ends on an eighth note; gently release this quickly.
- Kabalevsky deliberately introduces students to a double sharp in measure 14.
- Make the most of the dynamic contrasts.

A Little Song (No. 2)

Practice and Performance Tips
- Do not take this rather sad piece too quickly, which would destroy its mood and essence.
- Practice hands separately, observing carefully the phrasing the composer has indicated.
- The melody is passed from hand to hand, beginning in the right hand.
- The melody should be slightly more prominent than the accompanying hand.
- The composer's marking of *dolce* should be respected; play this piece gently, with sweetness.
- Create the drama the composer intended by playing all the dynamic contrasts.
- The most dramatic moment is the move from *f* in measure 12 to *subito p* in measure 13.
- Use no pedal at all.

At Night on the River (No. 4)

Practice and Performance Tips
- This floating, lyrical, melancholy piece should never go beyond ***mp*** and should not be taken too quickly.
- By paying careful attention to the dynamic changes and the hairpin swells, a proper sense of phrasing can be achieved.
- There is a definite ternary form: three six-measure statements of the melody with a slightly different ending to each.
- The phrasing should be carefully attended to in both hands, with a slight lift between each phrase in the right hand.
- The ending should feel as if the music is drifting away. The boat has sailed into the distance and is only faintly heard.
- It is an option to add a natural sounding *ritardando* in the last four measures

Selections from *24 Pieces for Children,* Op. 39
composed 1944

Melody (No. 1)

Practice and Performance Tips
- Make a graceful phrase in both hands.
- Practice hands separately in making the phrase.
- If small hands cannot use the fingers only in the left hand to play *legato*, very sparing use of the sustaining pedal can be used to create the smooth movement from chord to chord.
- Note the dynamic contrasts, with a sudden ***p*** in measure 5, followed by a *crescendo*.

Polka (No. 2)

Practice and Performance Tips
- For the first time in the progressive order of the book the melody moves to the left hand.
- The right hand plays an accompaniment.
- Practice hands separately.
- Note the smooth phrasing in the left hand and the *staccato* markings in the right hand.
- Then slowly practice hands together, exactly retaining the articulation Kabalevsky has composed.
- The challenge is to combine playing the left hand smoothly and the right hand *staccato*.

Rambling (No. 3)
Practice and Performance Tips
- Note the combination of *staccato* and sustained notes (with *tenuto* markings) in the right hand.
- Practice right hand only, carefully playing the composed articulations.
- Play the *staccato/tenuto* combination in the left hand as if it were an eighth note followed by an eighth rest.
- Practice hands together slowly, executing all the articulation exactly as composed.
- Use no pedal at all.

Cradle Song (No. 4)
Practice and Performance Tips
- Both hands play the same notes, in octaves, throughout. First practice hands separately.
- Practice may begin at *mf*.
- After becoming secure in the piece, then play softly and gently, but steadily.
- Create the two-note slur with *legato*, with a very slight lift before the next two-note slur.
- Note the composer's tempo marking of *poco lento*.
- Think of the tempo as gently rocking a baby's cradle back and forth.
- Use no pedal at all.
- Possible slight *ritard.* in the final measure leading to the final note.

A Little Joke (No. 6)
Practice and Performance Tips
- A perennial favorite, with good reason, this capricious piece concentrates effectively on parallel motion between the hands.
- The melody is the same in both hands, and is marked by alternating two-note slurs and *staccato* notes, with *portato* notes at the cadence points. Care must be taken to differentiate these three touches throughout the piece.
- Although the only dynamic given is *mf* in the first measure, it makes sense to shape the dynamics in eight-measure phrases.
- The phrase at measure 9 could be played several ways. Two suggestions are to begin *f* and *decrescendo* to the end, or begin *mp* and *crescendo* to the very end.

Funny Event (No. 7)
Practice and Performance Tips
- The entire piece is constructed of two-measure phrases, with one hand imitating the other.
- Every note is played *staccato*.
- Note the accents on the downbeats of measures 1–8 and measures 17–24.
- There are three sections to the form: measures 1–8, measures 9–16, and measures 17–24 (repeat of measures 1–8).
- Though still *staccato*, the dynamics and texture are markedly different in the middle section.
- Your practice tempo can begin as slow as necessary to keep a steady beat.
- Gradually increase the tempo in your practice as you master the music, maintaining steadiness whatever the tempo.
- Your performance should be playful and witty, to reflect the title.
- Use no pedal at all.

March (No. 10)
Practice and Performance Tips
- This solo explores a single rhythmic figure throughout in two-note slurs. Keeping this figure precise while executing quick extensions and contractions in the hand make this piece a technical and rhythmic challenge for the novice player. Moreover, to give the right "swing" to the four-measure phrases, the tempo must be adequately brisk to propel the line downward in a tumbling motion.
- Notably, Kabalevsky places the slurs as the performer would instinctively play them—from short to long. Does this mean that the player should lift the hand after playing each dotted sixteenth? Perhaps! One way of performing this phrase is moving from the emphatic, outer fingers of the hand (5 and 4 in mm. 1–2) to the thumb and release the hand slightly between the slurs. The slight kick that this motion gives to the downbeat is satisfying and physically fun to play.
- A fast tempo allows the hand to flip along from slur to slur with a slightly detached touch between the slurs.
- This piece is very brief, and so possibly warrants a *f* dynamic throughout, as marked. However, the performer could experiment with a terraced dynamic plan as well: *f* from mm. 1–4; *p* from mm. 5–8; *f* from mm. 9–12; *p* and *crescendo* to the end from m. 13 to the end.

Scherzo (No. 12)

Practice and Performance Tips

- This short piece can create a brilliant effect.
- Because it is so short when played at a fast tempo, one might repeat the entire piece.
- Practice should begin hands together at a slow tempo.
- From the beginning of practice, learn the articulation with the notes.
- Note the slurred three notes in the left hand, answered by two notes marked *staccato* in the right hand.
- The contrast between the slur and the *staccato* creates the essential character of the music.
- Use no pedal at all.

Waltz (No. 13)

Practice and Performance Tips

- Throughout the right hand plays a melody, accompanied by the left hand.
- Practice the right hand alone to create a beautiful and flowing melody, playing smoothly, noticing the composer's phrasing.
- If played without phrase structure, this melody will not be what Kabalevsky composed.
- Also practice the left hand separately, keeping this simple accompaniment gentle and quiet.
- With hands together, let the melody in the right hand be slightly louder than the accompaniment in the left hand.
- Play this lovely, melancholy waltz with no pedal.

Jumping (No. 15)

Practice and Performance Tips

- The piece is almost hands in octaves throughout, but with the composer's brilliant and simple twist of delaying the first beat in one hand by half a beat.
- The left hand leads in measures 1–8 and measures 17–23. The right hand leads in measures 9–16.
- The trickiest spot is measure 9, when the lead switches to the right hand.
- The articulation is key to successfully playing "Jumping."
- Throughout, the notes of beat 1 are slurred to a *staccato* on beat 2, followed by a *staccato* on beat 3.
- Note the sudden change to p in measure 9, followed the *crescendo* beginning in measure 15.
- The tempo and the title of the piece are clear indications of its fun spirit.
- Use no pedal at all.

Clowns (No. 20)

Practice and Performance Tips

- Begin practice hands separately and slowly.
- Learn the articulation (slurs, staccato, accents) as you learn the notes and rhythms.
- Learning the articulation from the beginning will help you learn the notes and rhythms.
- The melody is in the right hand, played with slight prominence over the left hand.
- The left-hand *staccato* notes should be played with a light bounce.
- Exactly and crisply playing the slurs, staccato, accents and dynamics will convey the fun shenanigans of circus clowns.
- Use no pedal at all.

Selections from 35 *Easy Pieces,* Op. 89
composed 1972–74

First Piece (No. 1)

Practice and Performance Tips

- Make a graceful phrase in the right hand, and answer it with a graceful phrase in the left hand.
- Smoothly pass the phrase from the right to the left hand in measures 9–10 and 11–12.
- Note the progression from p to mf and back to p in this brief piece.
- Gently and gracefully cross the left hand over for the final note.
- Use no pedal at all.

At Recess (No. 4)

Practice and Performance Tips

- The piece is comprised of three elements: two-note slurs, *staccato* notes, and four-note phrases.
- Each element must be precisely played to create the playful spirit of "At Recess."
- Make certain to smoothly move from right hand to left hand in measures 8 and 15.
- Though played f, this piece still requires a buoyant touch.
- Practice slowly with both hands together.
- Use no pedal at all.

First Waltz (No. 5)

Practice and Performance Tips

- The melody is in the left hand throughout.
- Note that Kabalevsky has added *tenuto* stress marks to the melody.
- The right hand is accompaniment, and should be played slightly softer than the left hand.
- Practice each hand separately at first.

- Be sure to play a legato phrase in the left hand as marked, measures 5–8 and 9–12.
- Kabalevsky's tempo of *Non allegro* warns you not to play this rather sad piece too quickly.
- Use no pedal at all.

Light and Shadow (No. 7)

Practice and Performance Tips
- The "light" is the loud music; the "shadow" is the soft music.
- Notice the contrast between the *staccato* markings and those notes without *staccato*.
- Be careful not to play all notes *staccato*.
- First practice hands separately, slowly.
- Then practice hands together, slowly.
- Retain the composed articulation in your practice, no matter what tempo.
- Use no pedal at all.

Little Hedgehog (No. 8)

Practice and Performance Tips
- Notice that every note of the piece is played *staccato*, with the final three notes also accented.
- Kabalevsky has indicated *staccatissimo*, meaning extremely short, crisp *staccato*.
- Practice right and left hands separately, and initially at a slow tempo.
- The sudden p in measure 8 followed by the *crescendo* creates a fun effect.
- Use no pedal at all.

Song in Octaves (No. 9)

Practice and Performance Tips
- Kabalevsky is teaching at least three elements: *legato* fingers, phrase and ledger lines.
- The *crescendo* in measure 2 leads to a stress on the downbeat of measure 3, creating a natural phrase.
- The second phrase, beginning in measure 4, culminates in something akin to *mf* in measure 6.
- The p in measure 7 is a sudden change, *subito*.
- Because the hands are playing in octaves, it's easy to introduce the high notes on ledger lines in the left hand.
- The *legato* should be accomplished through the fingers; use no pedal.

Playful One (No. 10)

Practice and Performance Tips
- Gracefully cross the left hand over the right hand in measures 4, 6, 10 and 12.

- Practice hands together, first at a slow tempo.
- Notice the two- and three-note slurs that Kabalevsky has composed.
- Accurately playing the slurs as composed will make the piece "playful."
- Use no pedal at all.

Trumpet and Echo (No. 15)

Practice and Performance Tips
- The right hand is the trumpet and the left hand is the echo.
- The right hand plays f, with each note articulated and accented.
- In contrast, the left hand plays softly and *legato*, moving from note to note smoothly.
- The composer's marking *marcato* refers to the right hand only.
- Practice hands together, first at a slow tempo.
- Use no pedal at all.

Little Goat Limping (No. 19)

Practice and Performance Tips
- For this piece in 5/4 time signature, the composer has helped by putting in dotted bar lines to divide the measure into two groups: 3 beats + 2 beats.
- Find the natural lilt in this music in 5/4, with a stronger emphasis on beat 1, followed by a lighter emphasis on beat 4.
- Executing the slurs and accents as Kabalevsky composed them will create the character of the piece. We suggest playing beats 3 and 5 in the right hand in measures 1–3 with separation just short of true staccato.
- Notice how the composer decorates the melody a bit when the music from measures 1–4 returns in measures 9–12 with different slurring the second time.
- Use no pedal in this crisply rhythmic piece.

Trumpet and Drum (No. 20)

Practice and Performance Tips
- The left hand represents the drum throughout, which should be played *marcato* and very steadily.
- The right hand is the trumpet.
- Accurately play the two-note slurs in the right hand.
- Carefully and enthusiastically play the accents as the composers has indicated.
- Even though the piece begins f, in measure 13 the composer asks for even more volume.
- Use no pedal at all.

Brave Song (No. 23)

Practice and Performance Tips

- *Con fuoco* means "with fire."
- Practice should begin slowly before working up to a fiery tempo. Dynamics are always relative. Even though Kabalevsky asks for *f* at the beginning, he later asks for a *crescendo* and then *più f* (louder). Make sure there is somewhere to go in volume with your beginning dynamic.
- Kabalevsky plays with the relationship of major and minor with the E-sharps and E-naturals in measures 9–12.
- Notice the strong accent on the syncopated left hand note on beat two of measure 17.

The Little Harpist (No. 24)

Practice and Performance Tips

- As the title indicates, this music imitates a harp.
- It is crucial to play the composer's phrasing, passing the phrase from hand to hand.
- A traditional technical approach would be to practice slowly, deliberately playing non *legato*, making each sixteenth note very even.
- Follow the above by playing smoothly and elegantly, but attempting to retain the evenness of the sixteenth notes.
- As the music is mastered, the tempo can increase.
- Practice without pedal. Kabalevsky (who often indicated pedaling in his piano music) did not mark any pedaling, a strong clue that he intended this little piece to be played without pedal.

A Merry Game (No. 26)

Practice and Performance Tips

- Kabalevsky uses the interval of parallel sixths throughout, until the final measure.
- Essentially, the left-hand note harmonizes the right-hand melody.
- Very exact pedaling happens briefly in measures 1–2 and 17–18.
- Except where marked, use no pedal.
- Carefully observe the articulations, whether *staccato* or slurred notes.
- The changes in articulation create contrasts essential to the music.

Stubborn Little Brother (No. 27)

Practice and Performance Tips

- The wit of this adorable piece comes from someone attempting to persuade sweetly, with a blunt response that refuses to comply.

- Through most of the piece (except for measures 18–20) the right hand plays smoothly and the left hand plays with strong *marcato* accents.
- Practice slowly hands together.
- The pedaling is by the composer. Pedal exactly as he wrote it, using pedal nowhere else.
- Be sure to release the pedal cleanly, exactly in the spot the composer indicates.
- Typical of Kabalevsky, the piece has many intricate details of articulation, slurring, dynamics and pedaling, all composed along with the notes.

Buratino's Dance (No. 28)

Practice and Performance Tips

- The character Buratino originated in the *commedia dell'arte*, a tradition of stock comic characters who improvised in traveling theatrical troupes. Buratino is also the main character of an Aleksey Nikolayevich Tolstoy's novel *The Golden Key*, or *The Adventures of Buratino*, which was based on the Italian novel *The Adventures of Pinocchio* by Carlo Collodi.
- Buratino is a wooden puppet or doll. The name is derived from the Italian word burattino, which means puppet.
- Imagine the jerky dance of Pinocchio in this piece.
- The two-note slur is the motive throughout.
- Kabalevsky challenges the student by hand positions changing frequently.
- Begin practice at a slow tempo, moving to a faster tempo as the music is mastered.

—Richard Walters, editor

First Piece
from *35 Easy Pieces*

Dmitri Kabalevsky
Op. 89, No. 1

At Recess
from *35 Easy Pieces*

Dmitri Kabalevsky
Op. 89, No. 4

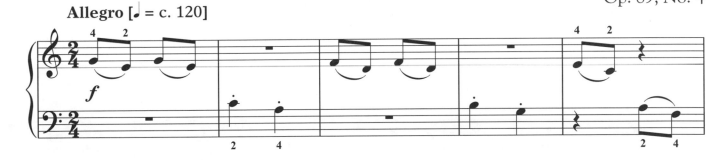

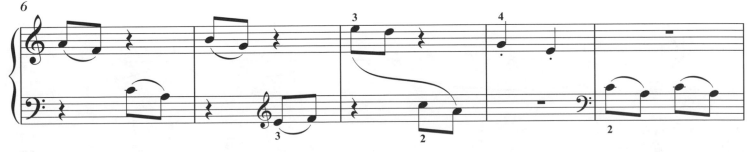

Melody
from 24 Pieces for Children

Dmitri Kabalevsky
Op. 39, No. 1

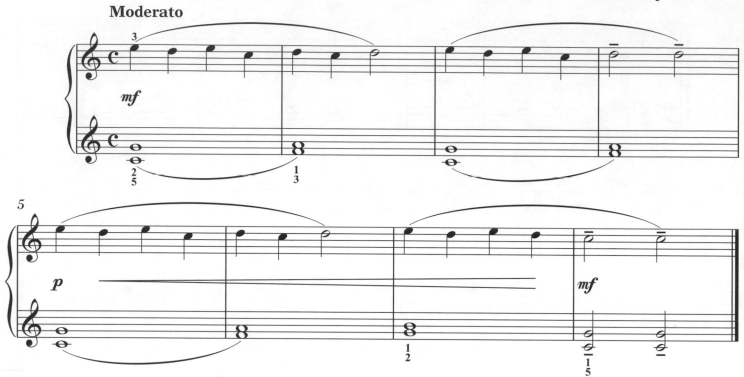

Polka
from 24 Pieces for Children

Dmitri Kabalevsky
Op. 39, No. 2

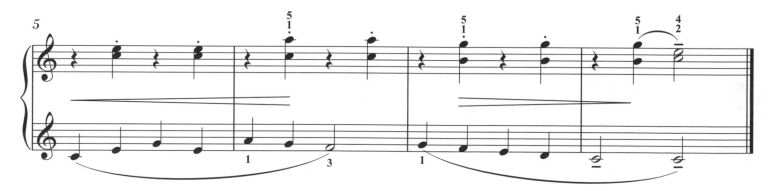

First Waltz
from *35 Easy Pieces*

Dmitri Kabalevsky
Op. 89, No. 5

Rambling
from *24 Pieces for Children*

Dmitri Kabalevsky
Op. 39, No. 3

Light and Shadow
from *35 Easy Pieces*

Dmitri Kabalevsky
Op. 89, No. 7

Little Hedgehog
from *35 Easy Pieces*

Dmitri Kabalevsky
Op. 89, No. 8

Cradle Song
from *24 Pieces for Children*

Dmitri Kabalevsky
Op. 39, No. 4

Poco Lento [♩ = c. 56–60]

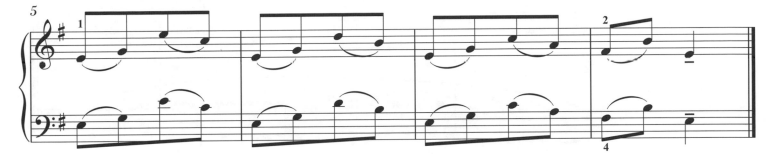

Trumpet and Echo
from *35 Easy Pieces*

Dmitri Kabalevsky
Op. 89, No. 15

Marcato [♩ = c. 112]

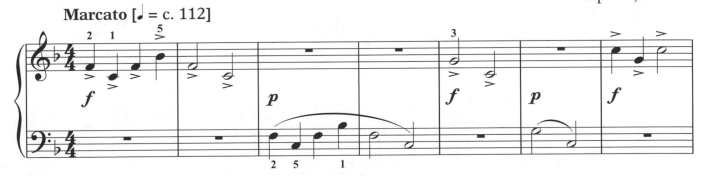

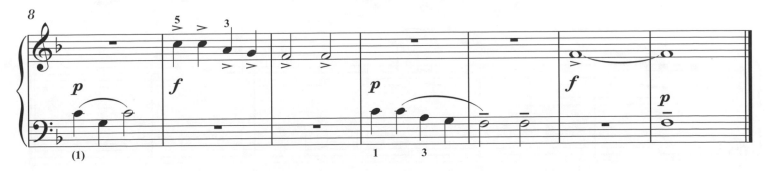

Song in Octaves
from *35 Easy Pieces*

Dmitri Kabalevsky
Op. 89, No. 9

Playful One
from *35 Easy Pieces*

Dmitri Kabalevsky
Op. 89, No. 10

A Little Joke

from *24 Pieces for Children*

Dmitri Kabalevsky
Op. 39, No. 6

Funny Event
from *24 Pieces for Children*

Dmitri Kabalevsky
Op. 39, No. 7

Moderato [♩ = c. 112]

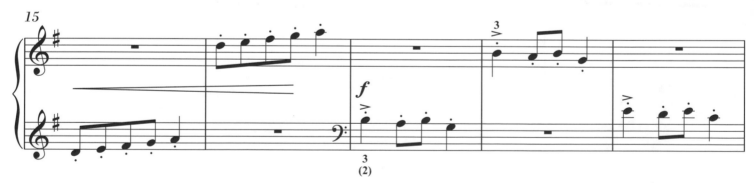

Little Goat Limping
from *35 Easy Pieces*

Dmitri Kabalevsky
Op. 89, No. 19

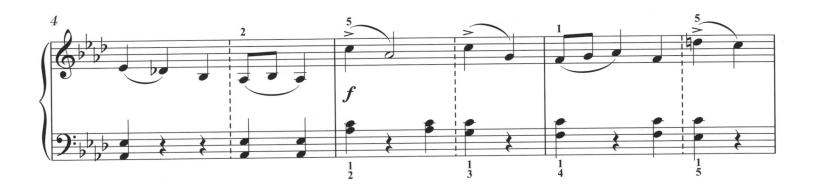

March

from *24 Pieces for Children*

Dmitri Kabalevsky
Op. 39, No. 10

Trumpet and Drum
from *35 Easy Pieces*

Dmitri Kabalevsky
Op. 89, No. 20

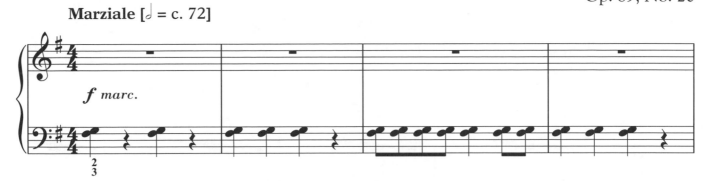

Scherzo
from *24 Pieces for Children*

Dmitri Kabalevsky
Op. 39, No. 12

Vivo, giocoso [♩ = c. 128]

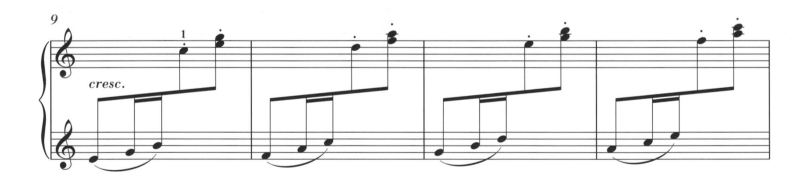

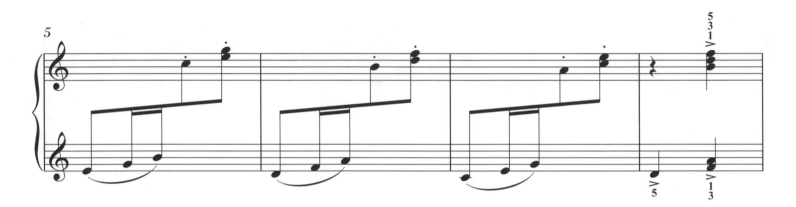

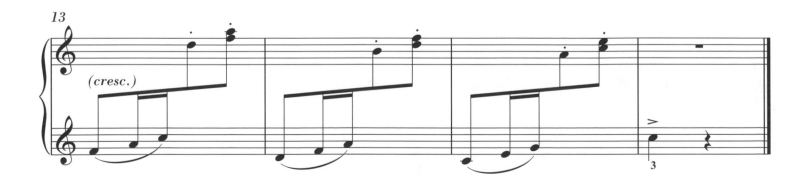

Brave Song
from *35 Easy Pieces*

Dmitri Kabalevsky
Op. 89, No. 23

Con fuoco

The Little Harpist
from *35 Easy Pieces*

Dmitri Kabalevsky
Op. 89, No. 24

Allegretto

(2)

Waltz
from *24 Pieces for Children*

Dmitri Kabalevsky
Op. 39, No. 13

Jumping
from *24 Pieces for Children*

Dmitri Kabalevsky
Op. 39, No. 15

Allegro giocoso [♩ = c. 120–132]

A Merry Game

from *35 Easy Pieces*

Dmitri Kabalevsky
Op. 89, No. 26

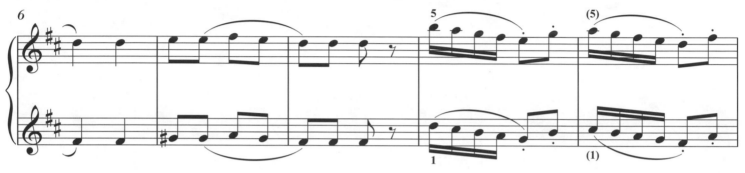

A Little Song

from *30 Pieces for Children*

Dmitri Kabalevsky
Op. 27, No. 2

At Night on the River
from *30 Pieces for Children*

Dmitri Kabalevsky
Op. 27, No. 4

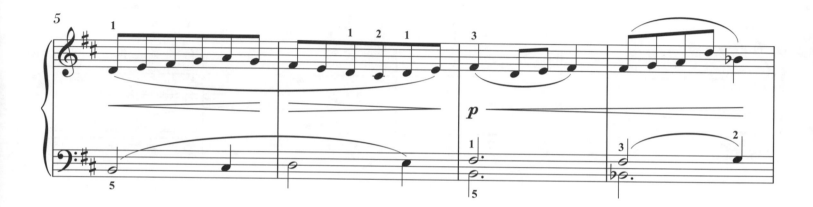

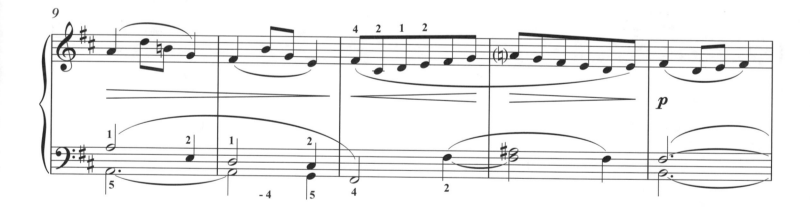

Stubborn Little Brother

from *35 Easy Pieces*

Dmitri Kabalevsky
Op. 89, No. 27

*Use fingers 2 and 3.

Buratino's Dance

from *35 Easy Pieces*

Dmitri Kabalevsky
Op. 89, No. 28

Allegro marcato

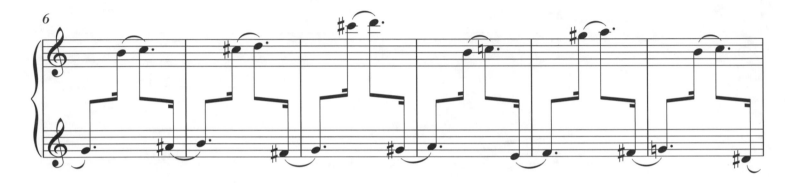

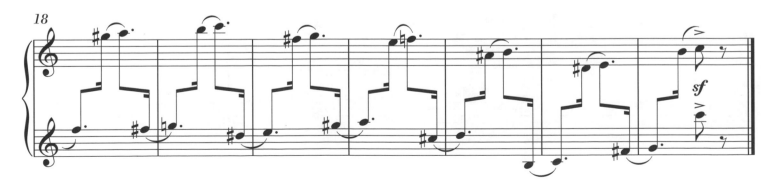

Clowns
from 24 Pieces for Children

Dmitri Kabalevsky
Op. 39, No. 20

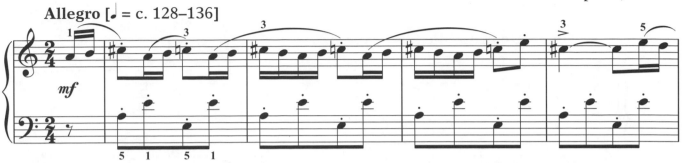

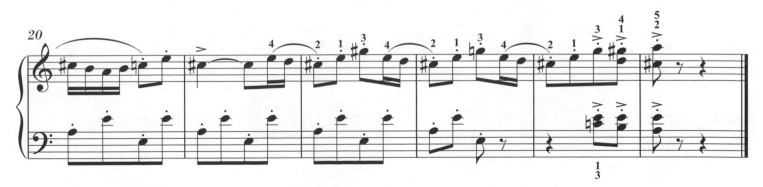

Waltz
from *30 Pieces for Children*

Dmitri Kabalevsky
Op. 27, No. 1

Allegretto cantabile [♩ = c. 108–120]

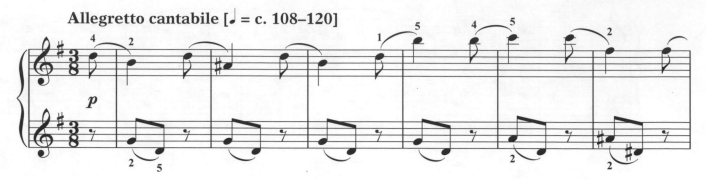

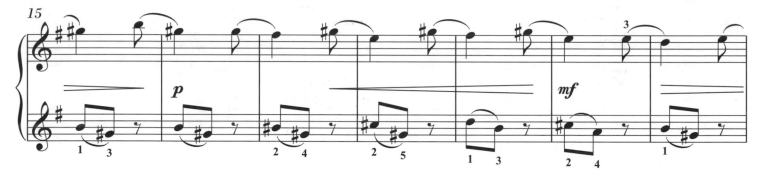